I'll Dress Myself in Wilderness and You

poems

CYNTHIA NEELY

Fernwood
PRESS

I'll Dress Myself in Wilderness and You

poems

©2026 by Cynthia Neely

Fernwood Press
Newberg, Oregon
www.fernwoodpress.com

All rights reserved. No part may be reproduced
for any commercial purpose by any method without
permission in writing from the copyright holder.

Printed in the United States of America

Page design: Mareesa Fawver Moss
Cover image: "Lake Linoleum," 2023 oil on canvas by Lindsay Breidenthal
Author photo: Dean Davis

ISBN 978-1-59498-195-1

Cynthia Neely writes stunningly of loss: the amplification of empty houses, the diminishment of metaphorical appetites, and most movingly—in "A Confession of Twenty-One Parts"—to her unborn. "Even when it's gone it lingers. / Even a body of water / skimmed with ice / still breathes." These poems with their twining of the Cascadia environment and the poet's own life are a gift. Neely has arrived at the important questions in her work: "Is this how the beginning ends?—A slow kiss / to another's sigh?" There's only one way to find out.

—SUSAN RICH
author of *Blue Atlas*

Compelling, elegant, and linguistically dynamic, *I'll Dress Myself in Wilderness and You* is filled with poems that perfectly balance emotion and intellect, painting intimate portraits of identity, loss, and nature. Neely showcases a true talent for imbuing the smallest human details with authenticity and layered meanings. Each poem maps out the human heart in relation to that larger earth heart in all their internal conflicts with precision and grace. With vivid and accessible language, *I'll Dress Myself in Wilderness and You* reminds us of the beautiful complexities of being human.

—JOHN SIBLEY WILLIAMS
author of *As One Fire Consumes Another*

I admire how these lyric poems take us so compellingly into the wilderness of bird and branch, boulder and snowfall, even as they take us into the wildness of the human heart. There is grief, a down-to-the-bone keening, and, in counterpoint, like music, love. The real thing. The baffling, messy, paradoxical, thin stubble kind. And I love that about this collection.

—DEREK SHEFFIELD
co-editor of *Cascadia Field Guide: Art, Ecology, Poetry*
and poetry editor of *Terrain.org*

"Sorrowing I love best. It sings like a saw," Cynthia Neely writes, considering the stages of grief. In spite of the personal tragedy at the core of *I'll Dress Myself in Wilderness and You*, Neely's newest collection overflows with profound reverence for all life—from people to pines and beetles to birds. In each poem she finds an original music to convey worry, self-doubt, loss, or enduring love, using a variety of forms that come together like one long ode to breath. A deeply honest, deeply moving, deeply beautiful book.

—SUSAN COHEN
author of *Democracy of Fire*

"It's not the leaving that's grieving me / it's all the grieving I'll have to leave behind," writes Cynthia Neely in *I'll Dress Myself in Wilderness and You*. Neely resolutely studies layers of grief: the loss of an unborn child, a world lost to climate change and fire, her son's retreat into divergent choices. All this and more is chanted in delicate form and craft, in ghazals and subtle rhyme. Deeply rooted in the Pacific Northwest, she continually finds wisdom in the living world—which, ultimately, becomes a mirror for our own suffering and survival. These poems find solace in connection with the land and with others but never deny the reality of longing.

—DION O'REILLY
author of *Sadness of the Apex Predator*

for Tom and Evan
the music in my life

Contents

Acknowledgments 11
   A Thing That Breathes 13
Breathe 15
   Ghazal to Breath 16
   This Loud Heart 17
   Etude 19
   Tonight, a blue moon rises 20
   Wheatfield with Crows 21
   Sunflower 22
   Elegy 23
   Since the return of the massasauga, ... 24
   So Much Depends on Hunger 25
   Apology 27
   Me Too—the Fall of Man 28
   What This House Knows 30
A Confession in Twenty-One Parts 31
   Hopewell Bay 32
Into the Wind 43
   Instinct 44
   Another Home 47
   Bittersweet 48

- Flashpoint 49
- Overseer 50
- Cast 51
- Dirge 53
- Nadeau Island, Shawanaga Bay 54
- Into the Wind 55
- That year, ... 56
- Let Me Swim 57
- Leap of Faith 58
- Not to Rise 59
- Wrecked 60
- Passing through Blue Earth 61

The Weight of Too Much Seeing 63
- Because Nothing's Ever Finished 64

As if the Whole Damn World Is Shining 69
- Not a Finch 70
- I Couldn't Name What Can't Be Named 71
- Today my son makes his first deep water dive, ... 72
- Cavern 73
- A Sturdy Well-Built Home 74
- My son is trying to forget himself 76
- Ghazal to No One 77
- Disembodiment 78
- Not as Beautiful 79
- At the end of February, ... 80

Surface Tension 83
- Forecast 84
- Finding the Words 85
- How Beautiful 86
- Aubade 87
- Home and Here 89
- The Cicada Heat of Summer Is Upon Us 91
- Edna Hid Walter from Us for Years 92
- One Story 93
- Surface Tension 95
- Color Theory 96

To My Mother While Listening to Stan Getz	97
What I Want	99
Bone Is Bone	101
Day 403	102
I'll Dress Myself in Wilderness and You	104
Note: "Because Nothing Is Ever Finished"	107
Title Index	111
First Line Index	115

Acknowledgments

Gratitude to the following journals and presses that previously published these (or versions of these) poems:
- *Belletrist*—"My Son Is Trying to Forget Himself"
- *Bright Hill Press—Like Light*—"Surface Tension" and "My Son Is Trying to Forget Himself"
- *Cutthroat Journal*—"Instinct," "Finding the Words," and "How Beautiful"
- *Floating Bridge Review/Pontoon*—"Forecast" and "Hopewell Bay"
- *Flyway Journal of Writing and Environment*—"Overseer"
- *Grabbed: Poets and Writers on Sexual Assault, Empowerment and Healing*—"Me Too, the Fall of Man"
- *Jet Fuel Review*—"Because Nothing's Ever Finished"
- *Measure, A Review of Formal Poetry*—"Etude"
- *MER—The Mom Egg Review*—"A Sturdy Well-Built Home" and "Apology"
- *Shrub-Steppe Poetry Journal*—"Another Home" and "Cast"
- *South Florida Poetry Journal*—"Not a Finch"
- *Talking Writing*—"Hopewell Bay"

Terrain.org—"I'll Dress Myself in Wilderness and You" and "I Couldn't Name What Can't Be Named"
Tilt-a-Whirl/Umbrella Journal—"Ghazal to No One"
What Rough Beast—"Not to Rise"
Women's Voices for Change—"Me Too, the Fall of Man"
Quills Edge Press—"Wrecked"

The following poems appeared as part of the Bright Hill Press winning chapbook, Passing Through Blue Earth (2016)—"Tonight a Blue Moon Rises," "So Much Depends on Hunger," "What This House Knows," "Passing Through Blue Earth," "Bone Is Bone," "Nadeau Island, Shawanaga Bay," "Since the Return of the Massassauga," "Home and Here," "Leap of Faith," "Sunflower," and "Hopewell Bay."

Seven Kitchens Press published the poem "Hopewell Bay" (2017) as a complete chapbook of the same name.

A Thing That Breathes

These are things you need to know:

someone will always outlive you
sometimes dogs howl just to hear themselves
sometimes you howl just to be heard
sometimes you disappear even as you are living

sometimes your body will betray you
multiplication deep in your cells
sometimes skin, sometimes bone
is not enough to hold you up

you have to have a mind of feathers
and see a bird in flight
to figure how it feels

to comprehend how simple
air can loft a thing

that breathes and bleeds and not to wish
for anything at all
but to be alone
in flight

with an eye turned only toward
the next the next and nothing

that could ever be
made different than it is

Breathe

Ghazal to Breath

The lake freezes, inhales, exhales, breathes.
At the dark edge, you will see it   breathe.

At the dark edge, you can fail, fracture, fall
without a sound or rise up, be free, resist,   breathe

without a sound. Can you hear it, see it, feel it, be
without meaning? Oh, be more, please, than this.   Breathe.

Without meaning, it still sings its warbling song, long, full.
A dark-eyed junco lives in a second's split,   breathes.

Your dark eye sees me as I am or maybe as I want
to be, rising up, reaching out, straining to   just breathe.

To be rising means you do not fall, you fill
with air, with hunger, with ache, you exist,   breathe.

With hunger, with ache, the dark edge seethes.
A frozen skim of skin rises,   breathes.

This Loud Heart

I could start
by closing the book
I never opened

I never opened
painted-shut window
I stayed closed

I stayed closed
cobwebbed concealed
I never spoke

I never spoke
the wanted words   no
I never opened

I never opened
my mouth to sing out
loud I never opened

closed my notes were
strange suspended
long wavering

harmony stretched
sustained elongated
I kept it in

I kept it in
all this fervor this
loud heart this

loud heart of steel
never stopped
anything

it never tried
anything
it ever tried

it feared
to fail to hold
so never opened

Etude

Music's in my blood, they'd hear me say
when anyone would ask about my need
to live my life a bird, that feathered cry
a part of me. A songbird's soul, a reed,
a silver flute. A constant metronome
of meter coursed my veins. And yes I breathed
it in and held it there, although my diaphragm
then pushed it out. A music that was heaved
upon a world I hoped would let me in
but kept me out. They tell me time will tell,
but then it won't. It keeps its secrets prim.
I learned to sing but didn't do it well,

my notes were strange. They didn't keep the time.
A crow subtracts its dark shape from the pine.

Tonight, a blue moon rises

and it's been years
since I've heard a fox

scream into the night
and wondered what living

thing was being either
ravaged or ruined.

I had no idea then
those sounds

were foxes, but now
I grieve their absence,

those nights of hunger,
heat so extreme.

Now I must be
content just watching

a blue moon rise,
listen instead

for the occasional
whippoorwill,

mourning loon, ceaseless
clock-tick in a windless dark.

Wheatfield with Crows

—for Vincent

A road lay where you lay, broken
by bent grasses trussed
to the scene by a crow-
filled sky, sanguineous visions

only you could see, looking
both backward and forward,
a singular perspective, dappling

stroke of wing and weather,
this black and blue sky/sea.
Oh Vincent. What hue did you see
in that Yellow House?

The wheatfield held a murder.
They say you bled out there.

And the yellow land erupted
with your black wings.

Sunflower

See how her face follows

                          the sun, somehow

turns from her western rest

                          looks east then straight

overhead, her heavy head

                          almost too much

on her spindle-neck

                          so simple, that summer

yellow, that seedy center

                          waiting to let go.

Elegy

No one there to see
the boys outside,
batter-up in grass-
stained jeans,
hat turned back.
No one there to hear
the crack of bat,
the crash of glass. Shards
drizzle down
like rain
on the Persian rug.
The yard un-mowed
since Tuesday-last,
papers piled
on the front
stoop, weeds
amid the peonies'
bowed heads.

Since the return of the massasauga,

I see snakes everywhere. Any whir
turns my head, any blur at the edge
of my vision. Sticks appear

to slither, leaves to whisper
without wind. It's the things we can't see
that get us—

the screwworm of boredom,
misshapen cells, hate that soothes
a seething soul.

Give me something
I can face head-on, a black bear
in the trail, not a tipped-black tail

disappearing into the brush,
hushed and shuddering.

So Much Depends on Hunger

—ending with a line from Sandra Alcosser

We are all born
into the yellow day

or the white-lit night,
hungry, rooting.

A man will lose a hand
to bring his family food,

a young girl braves the sting of stones
for her craving to learn to read.

Two women swing, shamed,
from brittle branches,

hanged for an appetite
not their own.

A wolf howls, her throat full
of quills white as rib bones.

While a coyote passes
the crevice-nest of vultures—

whose shadow-wings
mark the earth.

A fading snow-
shoe hare clenched tight,

she leaves the eggs
untouched.

So much
depends on hunger.

On the trail, a cougar watches,
tail tipped black and flicking,

while the deer barely lift their heads
from their fevered browsing.

Beyond the runneled peaks, clouds
wring the sun from the sky

as fall is upended, snow feathered
on stubborn aspen leaves.

The season's sewing its winter coat,
stitch by frozen stitch.

And ice gnaws
the riverbank, the river still swollen

from heavy rain, remade
each spring from snow melt

long before gentle grasses,
risen herons, silent water

slides—the color of a sky
I am told is filled

with the scent of wood smoke.
But I can't smell anything

anymore. I eat
but am never satisfied,

absence hollowed out
from a fullness in my throat,

every sucked-clean bone
a prayer.

Apology

My love   I don't know how   to tell you
what I know   how the sky   once blue
now like spillage   greasy and gray   might
one day have opened   and let you see
how rain is formed   the weep of it   now
I know   how they saw my face   shrouded
with a constant fury   now   how it urgently
mouths   *I'm sorry*   while clouds stumble
in skies where   once in a while bright and
heavenly bodies   have the audacity to rise.

Me Too—the Fall of Man

after the painting of Adam and Eve
by Peter Paul Rubens

Forgive me the need
to touch your breast,

though I did not ask,
and you did not offer.

Then, its ripeness
leaned in so close.

Begging for it.

You were reaching
for something. What?

Something more?
Some knowledge

new and shining,
daring and delicious?

Or some idea beyond
what you already knew

your life would be
here with me.

Why should I not, then,
taste as well?

Would you get on your knees
to only pray?

That he punished me too
is so unfair.

I told you it was a secret.
I told you not to tell.

What This House Knows

This house knows nothing
of the weight of words,
of books packed away

into lofty places. Snow,
oh yes, this it knows,
the measure of each flake

configured into truss and beam,
the wind shear factored,
the rain drained just so.

But this is what I understand:
an empty house is amplified, has more
to say than a filled one—

creak of floor, moan of tread,
groan of water pipe chanting,
chanting: *empty, empty*.

Today I rise no wiser.
How did I come to be
so vacant of words, images, care?

The house, in reply, cracks
and clicks, whispers and sighs,
a door closing.

A Confession
in Twenty-One Parts
(for a fetus at twenty-one weeks)

Hopewell Bay

1

a confession: I fell in love
with grief
not a single grievance
            grief

2

cisplatinum (cisplatin)

            a grievous but almost
            gorgeous word

liquid silver
iridescent
cool   as the water in this bay
            except it's

quicksilver   arrowed
            at fast growing cells

hot
unforgiving
            when it enters a vein

In vivo—
"within the living"
            it binds
            crosslinks DNA, triggers

apoptosis—
"cell death"

            3
                        I couldn't
                        warn you
to slow yourself
                        down
to settle your too-fast cells
                        into torpor
to forget your eyes
                        your ears
                        your fingerprints
skin

            4

malignant germ-cell tumors of the ovary
must be immediately treated
with combined chemo for at least three full cycles
(programmed cell death)

            5

Water [chameleon] takes on
            the color of its surroundings, so a body

            of it can be blue-sky, black-night, gray.
It can be scarlet as the cardinal flower it reflects or the star-

board buoy that marks the channel. Moss green
            as the grasses that edge the shore.

Grief. Like water. Moves
            changes
                        flows.
                                    Buoys me up.
You lived in water.

6
Water/Broken

Genus Laminaria—　　*green-brown kelp from the cold black*
　　　　　　　　　　 waters of northern oceans
Laminaria digitata—　*effective hygroscopic cervical dilator*

Seaweed
Devil's Apron
Sea Girdles

swells and swells and swells and swells and swells
five times its normal size to open the womb

Insertion
Dilation
Extraction

7

there are five stages　　of grief but only three stages of pregnancy

there are words　　　　for them　　we know
they say　　　　　　　 once through these stages we
let go　　　　　　　　　This is myth

8

There are five stages to grief but more words for grieving:

regretting
mourning
lamenting
languishing
aching
suffering
sorrowing

Sorrowing I love best. It sings like a saw
        —a poor man's viola.
It's not the leaving that's grieving me
        resonates like some banjo twang.
It's not the leaving that's grieving me—
        it's all the grieving I'll have to leave behind.

9

That black cat was ready to go, offered himself up
        to the coyote needing a meal.
The sorrel horse, flaxen mane flying, ready too,
        eyes feral, nostrils flaring.
The gray cloud of wolfish dog held on too long.
        My sorrow, I follow it
                      a faithful pet.

10

Worship it
this grief,
something to count on
like the scalpel, sharp   incisive.
Or that needle   impossibly long
that could reach the smallest part of me.

11

The world is scorching

around me
                a conflagration
                a congregation
of pines
                refuses to bow down
but still topples.

                Some ecosystems depend
                on spark and kindle.
                Some species must first bloom
                in flame to survive.

Balsamroot   bloomed
clustered   yellow-bright again
and so did I   pushing up
through   desiccated duff
all that   decay
waiting   for that flame
to burn   and burn.

12

A bag snags,
        fills with air on rusted wire
beside the high-plateau highway,
        the dust and rush of us
weighed down by what
        we cannot carry.
Who carried *this* emptied bag?
        What had it held?
A couple of steaks
        and a bottle of good red,
cast off sweaters for Goodwill,
        curtains for the new nursery,
a pregnancy kit?

13

Termination:

for medical reasons including medical illness in the mother is called "therapeutic"

Oxymoron:

an epigrammatic effect by which contradictory terms are used in conjunction:

living death
deafening silence
only choice
therapeutic abortion

14

  should I have   waited
          as if

a different answer could arrive

          not one
          deflated

  a scraped-out   womb

  fence-caught plastic bag
  when the wind calms hollowed

  red letters   distorted

  should I have waited
  dared the seething cells

  should I have waited
  to meet you   say
          goodbye

15

My grief
  is leaving me.
Twisting
  out of my grasp
even as I reach for something
  to hold, something to carry
and not let go.

16

I let you go

17

This summer's in a hurry,
moving off on a gust. My only son
wants to swim to Hopewell Bay.
Today. A round trip of a thousand breaths.
Alone. And I don't want to let him go
though I should know   no rotating prop
will dice him up   slice those lovely legs   rend
him piece by piece. He wants this test   his will
against my own.   Still
most days I would go,   match his stroke
for stroke,   breathe his breaths
if I could,   give my air
for him.   What is this giving in
resigned?   Where's my mean bone
now when I want it, gleaming,
gristled, unbending.

18

Should I apologize now
that I have almost stopped
mourning for what's been lost,
for what is leaving?

How the blue-gray umbilical
of memory holds
and holds,
and yet my grief is going   goes
the one thing I possessed
to keep you
clutched so tightly
to my breast.

If hope's a finch
that lightly touches down
    and leaves
the earth for sky,
then grief must be a hungry thing
that suckles and suckles
    and leaves
its mother dry.

19

I learned to say goodbye
(without saying anything)

20

Water's blue due to:

selective absorption
photon promoted transitions
highly excited vibrations, hues
observed as gray, blue/green, blue
light scattered by suspended matter

then returned to the surface.

21

There is evidence that fools us,
the blue of sky, the color of water.

There are things that we believe
without evidence at all—
God, karma, fate,
that a fetus feels no pain.

Even when it's gone, it lingers.
Even a body of water
skimmed with ice
still breathes
its skin rising and falling.

INTO THE WIND

Instinct

But it's not a bat that batters in
through the slightly opened slider
straight into the dog's mouth.
Rabies, I think too late and pull the dog away.

It was the light that drew it,
ceanothus silk moth, doe-gray, pinkish,
two black mock eyes and false ivory fangs
on wings of dust. Just a tinge
of visceral slime.

I pick it up, surely dead. Papery
wings spread the breadth of my hand,
the heft of desiccated leaf.

From her crushed thorax, a froth
of a hundred eggs or more. *No!*
I tell the dog. *No!* He wags,
waiting for the treat from my hand.

She must have felt my grief. Feathered
antennae suddenly swivel, downy legs
grasp air. I hope she'll fly and hold her
high out of the dog's reach

and over the fence. She flutters
and spins like an aspen leaf, falls
just on the other side. Still.

Then begins to crawl
up the chain link as if it were a branch
of ceanothus, fragrant and oily,
shiny and dense, and deposits the eggs
from her broken body.

What instinct drives us
to never give in before our journey's complete?
And what impulse makes some decide
to turn away?

She waited a long year to be here,
filled her monstrous grubby body full,
avoided being made a meal of, hibernated
cocooned in a silken pod as hard as plastic
to emerge for a day or two.

No mouthparts. Not meant to live.

So why then do I grieve her end?
Is it that she never fulfilled her purpose,
and so I mourn my own child lost?
Or is it simply seeing beauty crushed?
Seeing purpose and wanting crushed?

Whether we wake to birdsong or bullet fire
or news that fractures us, some
merely turn away, some drift powerless
against the current, some push hard
into the wind.

And I remember, each day,
the cells that should have killed me.
I remember each day
the child who died so I could live.

And each day I wake and worry
for my aimless only son. And I hear,
each day, another police shooting, refugees
drowned, another suicide bombing, and yet

I am still whole. And it seems I have no choice
but to be here to do what I do
with no good idea about why I do it.

I leave her on the chain link unmoving—a lone
leaf caught in fence-wire. A ruined moment
of compulsion. And then I recall the doe

on the road last night, just beyond
the circle of light, whose step becomes
a pirouette as she sees and turns away.

Another Home

Rotors thwap—a war zone here
in fire country
            —Sikorskys, Chinooks, smoke plumes
                    beautiful
as they are terrifying.
                    Blackened,
a snag still stands,   gutted,
now an osprey's perch—where he briefly rests
then plummets to the lake's surface,
catches water in the scoop of his hooked bill.

Three times
        he dips low,
slow like the plane that fills its belly
with river to drop on flames that color this land
charred, the sky sick
but stunning. Another home gone.
And we hope

            for a home to go back to. Tonight
the quarter moon shines through like faith
we must embrace

        while I ache
for the day I'll watch ice form,
each crystalline bit joining, conjoining, fogging
the mirror of the lake,

        and with necks outstretched,
swans, with their cygnets, will trumpet
and flap toward home.

Bittersweet

scarlet berries, showy, constant
in these Pennsylvania woods

where brilliant cardinals
perch and preen,

and although the pileated
pistons up each pock-marked trunk,

it's that lone leaf
vivid against dark bark

that gets to me,
spent but still hoping

for one last fair-weather day,
bittersweet

against the bitter wind

Flashpoint

Through the gag and cloy of spring
ceanothus—called snowbrush,
for her white blossoms—gasoline
bush for her inclination to leap
to flame at the first lick and flicker—

    the buzzards tilt and tip.

Spring—for now—but the earth is turning
to dust, balsamroot and lupine, phlox and paintbrush,
all seeking what moisture they can before
the last wilt of June becomes

    the tinder of August.

No one I know knows the flashpoint
where vapor will ignite in air,

the vulture's creviced ground nest vulnerable,
the coyote's den expendable.

One day I'll have to leave this place,
this place of our careful making,
front door ajar, food on the counter.
Save the dogs, leave the rest. Run
the well dry. Run.

One day fire will reclaim its lovers,
ceanothus, waiting with arms raised, open
and unafraid, ponderosa pine, Douglas fir.

    It will love them to their end.

No one I love knows how much
I love them. Not in the sense of spark and flame,
of all-in conflagration, no survivors.

Overseer

His skin was scabrous bark and thick
enough to tolerate the touch of men—
a torment of barbed wire
bound round twice and deep.

Yet he was victim, not to man
but to his age, the climate's change,
and beetles boring
in his spine. This pine

had lived on this steep hill
much longer than our cabin's stood,
oversaw its measured growth,
its rough-hewn logs a token to him

yet. The wind
came up too suddenly
and finally felled this sentinel.
History's written in the rings:

the drought of 1910
the burn in '48
the wildfires of '94.

Cast

The ravens on my mantle
are paired for life—are cast so
and so are too heavy for me

to carry from a home
that may soon fall to flames.

I am paired, like these birds,
with this house. Cast to it.
That antique desk, the stained-
glass window, Grandmother's
hand-carved tip-top table

can't be replaced, but the smoke-
filtered sun hanging low and red
over the mountain, the stone moraine
dumped and scoured—now lichen-dark,
a memory of the last glacier—
can't be scorched away.

Smoke that once smelled pleasant
as a campfire now reeks.
Stinks of sapwood and old duff
that didn't want to burn but has given in
too easily. I give in
too easily, will walk away
when once I thought I'd fight to stay.

This pair of ravens, bills gaped wide,
first carved in wax, then cast in bronze,
might survive a second firing, blackened
and burnished to an iridescent sheen,

as the living birds gleam
and rough their throat feathers,
croak and cough,
My place. Mine!

Dirge

I watch you die,
death by small death,
needle by needle,
blighted by drought,
a cast on the mouths
that feed on the light.

I touch the parched earth
you have tapped for your drink,
the dust and the duff
soft at your feet.

The wind has come up,
a gust oddly warm,
too soon in this month
and winter too thin
with March ushered out
before it's come in.

The signs of your death
now cover the ground
in light shades of gold
and red-tinted brown,
and I pray for some rain
so you'll still be around
come August.

Nadeau Island, Shawanaga Bay

Pines here bend

to the will of the wind,
north, south, east,

though west wind bends them best.

They begin their slant
as seedlings, barely

there, in meager crevices,

eager in pink granite,
hardly enough soil to set in,

yet root they do

and take their shape
despite what we may want for them,

a tall life, unbent, unburdened.

My son adrift
doesn't discern my wishes—

strong strokes in his own direction.

I cry out warnings over
the broad, bright bay.

The wind just carries them
away.

Into the Wind

On the paddle to Flat Rock, an island hanging
smooth on the edge of the open water, water-

snakes coil, uncoil, drift like rust-stained rope lost
by some other passing paddler. Terns shriek and dive.

A bittern drips its dripping-faucet-at-midnight noise,
turns bill toward sky and weaves like wind-swayed reeds.

All this has been here when I have not. I hope it will
be here when I have gone. Each small bay I used to claim

as my own now seems to show some sign, perhaps of those
like me, who've handled rocks and built their cairns

to leave their marks where they should have only drifted through
like this pair of loons and flightless fledge who chuckle

and hoot their warning hoots—they will be leaving soon,
will leave their too-late young—while two great blues

croak displeasure at surprise and, hump-necked, rise,
thumping, thumping, into the wind.

That year,

death wintered over in me
like an animal.
Spring was hard
coming. Summer slower
still. That year the world
seemed loud, indiscernible,
inexplicable, unmoving,
unlike the river flowing still, still
carving its way around or through
each obstacle, each design of nature
or mistake of man. Does the river rise
to meet the dam? Or is it forced
into submission, tamed, tired?
Now the idea of ideas is dying
a difficult death. Like the moths trapped
in the pantry traps, sticky and fragrant,
like the boy's pet cat, coyote-cornered,
no escape.

Let Me Swim

If the dying
      move through memories

like fish muscle through water,
      and death's simply a function

of the body—lovely
      and messy, its beautiful

arithmetic, measured
      breath amended—then

someone always holds
      too tight and releases too late,

the fly-caught trout, needing
      to capture the image

when the pitiful thing can
      no longer breathe.

If death is drowning in air—
      one last tail-slap,

eye-bulge, gill-pulse—then
      death, when you come,

let me swim to you instead.

Leap of Faith

> *Some species of spiderlings use airborne dispersal to vacate the area where they have hatched, hanging on to a loose strand of filament in the wind. Sailors have reported spiders being caught in ship's sails over a thousand miles from land.*

Mid-lake in midair,
a spider's silk
floats, cast
on a breeze's spasm.
The spider, too,

carried along
on faith.

Then, in a slant of light,
the glisten of a thousand threads.
How long must this kind of crossing take?

When do they decide
they are far enough away

from the one whose body
carried them?

This is not Kierkegaard's leap, I know.
Even as they're holding on,
they are letting go.

I paddle on, still hold to hope
that some might ride along,
be this way borne to shore.

Not to Rise

What seeds take root in the crevices of your mind?
Not holy or wholly formed around the edges,

not a sideways glimpse of swallowtails or finches,
not jazz or jelly roll or belly laugh you'd only find
naked as a myth—not truth.
                        Time's thankless pendulum
swings, your pericardium cracks again, brings
you to your knees. Your heart's a bird that sings
though it's never known the sky. The humdrum
evening stings.
                        You know it's time to exorcize
these weeds propagating in your skull. Star
thistle, knapweed, salsify.
                        My God, how far
away it seems, the calm of night, the bedsheets' sighs.
You want the day to be embalmed, to end
but not to rise again.
                        To sleep to sleep to sleep   and

Wrecked

> *upon witnessing a mass grounding of the tiny blue jellyfish,* Velella velella, *on a beach in Oregon following news of the disappearance of Malaysia flight 370 with 239 people on board*

Did they suffer?   That is always the question
when lost   blown out of the sky
failed by the wind.

Velella velella   we "by-the-wind sailors,"
sand in the crepe of our windward wings
such things we've seen   fair-weather fuselage

hell-hull of rust   the sea's bright stars too
fallen lifeless   limbless

blue-boated and silver-sailed   bloated
with salt and sea   we go
where the surf has pushed us   stranded
when the tide goes out

Did we suffer?   Was it pain we knew?

You search for wreckage
then search the wreckage for clues

Passing through Blue Earth

—a town in Minnesota
a white and black cloud

pelicans against eggshell sky
looking for something

the color of water
to settle on

no blue earth
as far as I can see

as far as I can see
rust-tinged tarmac

lolls like a tongue
oozing its hot breath

into the too-hot air
all the way to the red earth

of the Black Hills
and I worry

for the orange tabby
mousing in the median

the rough-ribbed deer
browsing the brown shoulder

I worry
for the lone and lonely

gray roan in the once-green field
missing a herd it never had

the rag of roadside coyote
her blind and orphaned litter

the fires at home
polar bears

the rain forests
my drifting son

this blue planet
this sweet sphere

this perfect earth

we are all just
passing through

The Weight of
Too Much Seeing

Because Nothing's Ever Finished

—a cento series from Jane Hirshfield's "The October Palace"

They Opened, Because It Was Time and They Had No Choice

They open their skin at first touch, yielding sweetness.
Ripeness is what falls away with ease.

The mouth swallows *peach* and says *gold*.
What enters, enters like that—unstoppable gift
because you taste it as you were meant to.

~

Sunlight Never Reaches but the Earth Still Blooms

cobbled and rivered with all the green waters of earth,
the taste of things, cold and pure,
the murmur of falling, the fluvial, purling wash,
the steep descent tasting of oceans,
the merest trace of sorrow, remnant salt,
the beating, breaking, scoured-out chimes of wave-scrub.

From glacier-lit blue to the gold of iguana,
a shiver of crayon yellows and reds, of violet
on stone-colored ground.
All day the world went on about its business.
I must have missed it.
Even the silkworm's castings grew whiter, more strong.

~

For Fish, Water Is Endless, for Birds, the Air

open-winged for those moments between world and world.
We name them, and naming, begin to see.

The deep fish rise to feed as if some riddle
assembled on thread so fine it is almost surmise,
though a shadow flickers, remembering.

They are fish going on with their own concerns.

~

Would Tenderness Wring the Heart Still of Its Burdens

leaving only the dark salted circles
yellow, plump, a little bruised?
The smooth and the scabbed, the wrinkled and lonely?
Each answer known before the question's asked.
Ideas buzz the air like flies,
a plentitude that binds.

Again, the Wind Flakes Gold Leaf from the Trees

as these falling needles and leaves speak of return.
The poor had returned to their hunger,
more and more creased each year, worn paper-thin
in steady homeward weatherless migration
to be pounded down again for what we've declared beautiful to be,
each half-starved rib communicative as Braille.

I too now wear that warning and so pray
it is possible to cast yourself on the earth's good mercy and live,
each of us pinned on the axis that spins out this dusk,
the night's stampede of winds.
Only the wild scent of the earth will be left,
and the angels look on, observing what falls: all of it falls.

Today, What Falls Is Wavering

from the weight of too much seeing, too much seen.
Each time the found world surprises—that is its nature,
moving of shadows and grass
in their sweetness and rustling.

Now see the dark-shelled flowers of thought unmade,
its many shades of gray.
These thought are yours—though I wish they were mine.

Whatever Asks, Heart Kneels and Offers to Bear

Why does my heart look back at me, reproachful?
Fold that loneliness, one moment, two, love, back into your arms.
Like new lovers taking their fill in the crowded dark,
their shadows' chiasmus will fleck and fill with flies.

Such is the chaos that affection yields.

The heart's machinery starts up again, hammering and sawing,
humming of flies on their isinglass wings.

Then it asks more, and we give it.

As if the Whole Damn World Is Shining

Not a Finch

Your son wants to be
a fish,   not a finch,

to dive deep below fogged surfaces,
dark-scaled   and glistening.

No matter the color
of the day   its crystal

sky   the water
the color of moss

and memory.
The call you want to hear?

That sound of spring
and gladness?   Absent.

The wings that quivered
to stroke flight   you bound

by too-tight loving,
too late given.

Your son wants to be a fish,
not a finch. Because   you see

in every bright-winged thing
such promise.

I Couldn't Name What Can't Be Named

Because the end of the day looks like diamonds
adrift and nestled on needles
of the tallest trees.

Because my ashes will settle like that
late afternoon light, then sift
with the wind.

Because when the wind shifts,
I fall again.

Because, in time, I regret everything,
apologize for nothing.

Because my son's mind is not a question
for which I have an answer.
A punctuation mark
without conclusion.

Because we always try to name
what can't be named,
we label the constellations
so, in naming, we might remember.

Because we can't carry the light
of a million fallen stars:

the belt and shield of the hunter,
the mother bear and her son,
the tail of the scorpion that could kill him.

Today my son makes his first deep water dive,

the child who so loved water, he didn't want to be born,
insisting that he'd rather be anything but normal,
no, no typical drum. Swallowing words, I'd watch,
years later, his impossible mission to catch
something miraculous, the gulls swept in
his wake, he an otter in the bay, thoughts kept in
his water-slicked head, all the mysteries there
in deep water. If I relent and ask him where
he's been, he doesn't answer. Says, hey, I'm alive.

Cavern

Each spring I watch   the cowbird
                        steal a nest, lay a solitary egg
next to those of warblers or finches
who raise the chick as their own
                   eaten out of house and home,
                   and I think of my son,
his mouth still seeking sustenance,
his arms still reaching,
                   his too-small shoes still closeted
                   with too-tight shirts
and too-short pants that tell me again
I couldn't feed his hunger, tell me again
                   I couldn't sing him happy or full.

A Sturdy Well-Built Home

For weeks we'd watched the white-headed male
whittle our porch post, the rotting wood irresistible,
for a nest that might befit a mate. Tempting her
with a tapped-out invitation, pulled in by the promise
of a flawless home.

We listened, hushed, at the first pale squeaks and hisses,
here from our perfect perch to witness the metamorphosis
of bright white egg to fully fledged flyer. Nothing like *this*
creature, still not stiffened, translucent in the driveway.
Gripped for weeks by some sad sleepiness, I woke, at last,

to a brightened world, finally seeing the glacier lilies'
yellow nodding heads, the sprouting spring beauties
in their lacy go-to-meeting caps. I see the spotty fawn
no bigger than a tabby cat, no more than a morsel
for a mountain lion, maybe just enough
to feed a coyote's pups for a day.

I see again the vibrancy of living
in a home surrounded by nature—life and suffering,
beauty and fear. And here the awkward chick,
flaccid in the driveway, much too far from its nest
to have flung its own fragile body there.

Pushed or carried out? Fallen or torn away?
Not quite cool in the lightly closed warmth of my palm,
my tepid breath breathed into its pale, slack bill.
Transparent flesh, all internal organs visible.
Membranous bulges where eyes would soon have been.

Like a fetus at twenty-one weeks,
a child aborted. His body's home unwell.
His mother forced to fling him from this womb.
Grief, why do you visit me these ways?

Some birds mate for life despite their losses, return
to the same place to try again. So we, too, tried again,
revamped the nest, forgiving and plump,
a sturdy well-built home. But now our only son
has my disease, one that ceased our first hope's forming.
Our home, our carefully crafted home, is not as safe

as it would seem, the nest hole filling with a freezing rain.
All that effort, raising young to autonomy, drowned.
Posts replaced, the birds no longer scold us for our spying
or peer at us to grasp our true intentions. No longer labor
in frenzied unison

to keep their only hatchling fed and sheltered,
to keep their only offspring safe from the world.

My son is trying to forget himself

—after a line from Lynn Emanuel

and remember himself as someone else
who can find gladness in shadows, lightness
in despair, face gone blue
in monitor-shine, conquering the cellar
of his own desires. Lovely, dissatisfied man-child,
content in his own unmaking. I remember us
at the stubborn table, dinner uneaten, and then the words
that can't be stuffed back down my throat,
and I see his fear—that he does not want
to be like me, his fear that he is
too much like me, his fear that he might never leave
this soft flab of home.
I have loved him all his life,
dedicated myself to the act itself.
I have handed him the plate
from which he will not eat.
I have handed him the plate,
dedicated myself to the act itself.
I have loved him all his life,
this soft flab of home
too much like me, the fear that he might never leave
or be like me, his fear that he is.
And I see his fear—that he does not want,
that can't be stuffed back down my throat,
at the stubborn table, dinner uneaten. And then the words,
content in their own unmaking. Remember us,
of your own desire, lovely, dissatisfied man-child,
in monitor-shine, conquering the cellar
in despair, face gone blue.
Who can find gladness in shadows, lightness,
and remember himself as someone else?

Ghazal to No One

They said, and she believed, no one knew.
No one knew

when it was there. When it wasn't there,
no one knew.

When she asked them what she should do,
no one knew.

When the snow fell, pure and white,
no one knew

there was crimson there. Forceps, curette, oh
no one knew.

Opened, emptied, no sweetness left, no,
no one knew

she despaired the lack, the slacked belly.
No one knew.

When her husband wept without a sound,
she never knew.

Disembodiment

body from body	water
breaking, flesh	quickening
	hour's incessant dangling
a moaning	a deluge
knuckles	a tiny hand
a cloudburst	crimson gush and cry
a tongue	that I don't understand
	I can't unravel
a son	I fail
I do not embody	motherhood
	its truth or calm
am not the nesting starling	compelled by devotion
	to feed the cowbird's chick
not the snarling bitch in whelp	
	keep away keep away
I embody something other	other than what I need
what I need	I need
oh to be fierce	oh to be smitten
what I want	I want
I want	what is lost

Not as Beautiful

They tell me my uterus
is only for show, unless

                                      someone else inhabits it.
Someone did, more fish
than child, until

                                      he wasn't. Over-ripe
peach, lotus blossom,
sea creature, gilled and glorious,

                                      beloved and buoyant.
Who says I did not
love him? Even as needle

                                      found his heart
an iridescent hummingbird's bill
plunged deep to nectar. But

                                      not as beautiful.
Forgive me I say
each day to the emptiness

                                      —*my* womb
but not to those
who pray for me

                                      to perish
instead.
My life

                                    for yours, my love.
Maybe one day
I can say

                                      I know you
Wild honeysuckle climbs
to reach the sky

                                      but never will.

At the end of February,

the storm has finally come
amidst the promise, packaged
as warning   global warming

—and I'm in awe
of its irony—
ten feet   in ten days

yet still not as deep
as in that photo—a still-young
wolfy dog in a heavy coat

dwarfed by boulders
dwarfed by their own
thick coats   of crystalline white.

Our son sits   wide-eyed
in a pack on your back,
and I suppose I am behind

the camera   taking it all in
like a mere observer,
not a mother   a wife,

a guardian—snow is
such pure perfection,
but it's not meant to last—

it slumps   gray and cold,
that old dog will hold on too long,
as our son someday leaves us

without words.   But today,
today the sun shines through
snow balancing on branches

like through the feathered
edges of clouds,
like a beam of torchlight held

to our son's small hand—
it shines   it shines
as if the whole damn world
is shining.

Surface Tension

Forecast

Confused weather. Look out
over the bay after the daylong storm
which should have cleared the air
but didn't.

If I wasn't seated, tethered by this chair
to this granite island, I could believe
the way upward and the way downward
are the same. Perhaps I believe that
anyway. I write

here in lantern light, well past midnight,
while the waves that wander in to shore
offer no reprieve. Not a single simple breeze
disturbs this fog—almost
a porcelain feel—

brittle, like it might craze, crack,
like that plate that hit the wall.
You might recall that night,
the storming off. We are
altogether too much
weather.

Finding the Words

I've been imagining my death
again. The man   boy really

with the gun   stunned
by his own presence,

fresh from war or wounded
by love   or hate

seems fated to take this step
since he first walked

between his father's
grasp to his mother's

grin, all the hope open
there. And here

he is. The bullet
takes out my throat

so I can't speak, I can't
say what I have always wanted

to say. My husband will later
discover my poems

and finally find the words
that he's been missing.

How Beautiful

I find the long braid while cleaning out a drawer.
Same shade and smoothness as back then
in that borrowed station wagon, his long hair
hiding his face as he bends to the neck of his first love,
his guitar, and I begin to adore his chords, his hands,
how they move. And he falls in love
with my long, shining hair.

The day I start chemo, I know it will go. But it's weeks,
and I begin to pull hope to me, to hold on to it
with a fierceness I didn't know I had. It's almost
waist-long, until handfuls later I take the shears to it.
Gather it together with a band into a long tail and cut, cut, cut.
So thick the scissors won't go through.

This is not the beginning of my being a foreign body,
a body foreign to me, to him, to any of the doctors
or techs who treat me, and I think I am resigned to it.
Still, I save this shining skein and can't recall doing so.

But I do remember he comes home one night
and shaves my head, kisses the thin stubble of it, tells me
how beautiful it was, how beautiful it is.

Aubade

To begin with the end, what the rain
    did not uncover. A teacup overflows,
we call it a spill; a riverbed overflows, we
    call it a flood, what it is to be swept away.

—Kate Willingham, Darwinist Logic on Unrequited Love

Up north

where my summer skin first lay touching yours,
a whitethroat calls until the last shards of light
fall from between the branches,

and all that remains
is shadow cast by the moon
reflecting off the bay.

I beg for a breeze or your caress, restless
without you. A spider seems to free fall, spinning,
legs outstretched as if to slow her plunge. Her web,

cornered in the window's wooden frame,
is perfectly designed, methodical, defined, but
unsafe from the uninvited who fray her fabric
and begin her downward drift.

Is this how the end begins?—soft,
amorphous, long before the division
of assets, the taking and relinquishing

like a hot day that gives in to evening's cool,
not wishing to fight it anymore? Sodden, saddened.
Is this how the beginning ends?—a slow kiss
to another's sigh?

I wake from my dozing to the rolling of thunder,
rumbling off this granite island's floor, and to the rain
borne on the wind through the window above our bed.

The storm passes directly overhead, quieting the early birds,
sending beetles to seek shelter, beside the hint of first light,
between the battered boards of this cabin's walls.

The rain moves off along the archipelago
to erase the eastern shore, blots the glow
that's making morning there. A promise

hangs in the air somewhere, tenuous
and tenacious as a spider's silk repaired by dawn,
the finishing touches tended to as day begins to break.

And the whitethroat takes up its call,
sings: *Can-a-da Canada Canada Canada*

Home and Here

This morning, fog
hangs so thick it sticks
to the surface
of everything, everything

sopping in this glorified
shed called cottage
on this far-flung granite island,

while at home, fire burns,
brings the forest to its knees
in prayer for a little bit
of this mist.

Home and here.

These are the places
that pull me by each arm
like quarreling parents.

Twin Sisters, who inhabit
the horizon, disappear,
nearer islands too, and my father

is foolish, out in the boat
on some task mistaken
for important.

Mother and I

fret for his return,
her aided ears unable
to detect the dim and distant

hum of outboard
negotiating shoals in
the narrow, socked-in channel,

her footsteps
restless in the dance
of sixty-three years.

My husband, too, waits,
home, worrying
over fire and my return,
as I wander lost

over rocks and moss and ponder
how I will find my own way
back home.

The Cicada Heat of Summer Is Upon Us

Seventeen years
is buzzing up
in the oak treetops.
Tell me luck
is with us
on the wind,
a breeze to ease
the stifling heat,
nil the stillness
in the air, drive
the moisture
from my hair.
Father, Mother, God—
a Christian Science prayer.
Sing the odd
cicada song.
Up from dirt,
arisen from sin.
From tail to eye,
shed my skin,
live to die
but sing to live.

Edna Hid Walter from Us for Years

My mother's father
was allowed to say hello,
to smile and ask our names,
again, to ask us what we do—

Are you the photographer?
then haul out the Zeiss,
fumble with it, mumble
about how it used to be
easier to comprehend.

My mother's mother's deepest fear
was people would discover
what she hid from us for years.

To her chagrin,
his sin was fog. A curse.
The purse of his mind
open and upside down.

One Story

This story starts in Toronto, where an orphaned son
meets a girl who is kinder than anyone
he's ever met. Kinder than the blood uncle

who would not take him in, kinder
than the family who took his sister
but did not take him, kinder

than his adoptive father whose obsessive need
to be loved by children he may or may not
have grasped. Or maybe the story rises like a spell

in a kitchen, warm with the scent of baking bread,
and a wife who greets him there and cups him to her
with towel-dried hands to sway wordless.

This story sustains an island-studded bay,
a blue hand-built sailboat with Egyptian
cotton sails and wine-red mahogany brightwork,

where the wind yodels like loons or huffs like otters
whose broad tails barely leave a wake, and the horizon
never gets any closer no matter how far or fast you go.

And this begets another story:
a child who wants to know what it's like
to be a boy, who tries to stand

to pee, who sets her turtle free
in the vacant lot next door, draws palominos
because she can, rides a bike named Fury

and tames, with a chitter, every bird
and squirrel in the neighborhood. Maybe
this story takes place in Pennsylvania,

Vermont, Connecticut, Washington, Ontario,
on the back roads, on the mountain passes,
or on the smooth-rock islands. Any wild place.

The girl with a boy of the untamed, the woods,
a mountain climber, a boy who became a man
who stayed. Or maybe this story tells of a girl

who wondered what it would be like to be a boy
but who became a woman who, when she finally
conceives, learns she can't keep her child.

Or is it a story of a mother who
finally has a son, all hope answered, but
can't save him—or the pygmy owl, the sparrow,

the nuthatch that didn't understand the lie
of window's glass. The story will go on,
even as the wasps stumble, roused from winter sleep,

as the spring beauties raise their pink-brocaded heads
and as the orphaned old man loses the vision in his left eye,
forgets his father's secrets,

lets go his hand-built sailboat, his good eye
still on the horizon.

Surface Tension

The sink attracts them.
Toothpaste I think.
They crawl in but can't climb out,
and I watch one struggle, glued
by surface tension on his brown beetle-y back.
The effort to right himself thwarted.

A run of toilet paper. Three sheets
laid into the sink and out
over the rim. He hooks one barbed leg
for purchase, flips himself
right side up, scrambles straight out.

At night now, to avoid a basinful,
I leave the ladder down
so they'll be gone by the time morning
pierces the cracks of the cabin's walls.

I can't seem to find pleasure
in washing them down the drain.
They just crawl back up again anyway.

I read somewhere they can survive
underwater for days at a time,
even gill-less, even lacking
an umbilical connection to blood and oxygen.

My father, who is not a cruel man,
flushes them with boiling water,
like tiny crustaceans. But I imagine
their miniscule screams.

Color Theory

In the Painted Hills,
I wonder, before God

picked up his paintbrush,
if he studied color theory,

and where he hid his mistakes,
or did he simply cover them

over again. No need to keep
the evidence around.

To My Mother While Listening to Stan Getz

Mother, may I write of you now—
how the shades of the seasons flushed
full in your hand, your brush fine-stroking
the patterns of your perseverance,

the unfinished still
on the easel?

Forgive me.

I never wrote a poem to you, and still
I write of your husband, my father, ruined
canvas, paling in your absence.

When he agreed to let you go,
and you said *thank you, darling*,
did he know they'd be your last words

to him? That you'd speak to each
of us, in order of birth—your children,
always your finest unfinished works.

How would he know *make me beautiful*
would be your final request—perfection
to him for more than seventy years.

That my sister would be the painter,
soft brush of blush and lip tint, essence shining through
patina of skin and bone and tubes and pain,
my father—head-phoned, eyes closed.

I think even then you knew I would still be writing
of him—his loss of you. His loss of him.
Mother, may I

listen with your husband to that jazz, bright and blue,
that you could never hear, your aided ears unable
to take it in, his pleasure and his pain, the sound reedy
but full, horns moaning, crying out?

What I Want

All last night the wind
told me spring was heading out—
the marmots have birthed their young,
the balsamroot are all beheaded,

the red-tail's belly's full.

And I despair spring's passing
just as I will summer's end
and autumn's last leaf too. Still
today I mourn the absence of snow.

I watch my father falter.

In the end, the tales of those
that have been told,
are those then tethered here?
Or are they ethered into air?

I can't even see you
my dad says when I ask him
to notice I'm distraught. His answer
to any question—*I don't know*.

Neighbor, John, wanted to die
on this mountainside, which he did
after too many seasons to count.
Do we ever truly welcome what we want?

what I want is to know my child is sheltered
what I want is to know my child
what I want is
what I want

When I lose my grasp,
will it be too late for me to ask—
what will hold our stories?

Wind might hold to mine.
The wind from the west that bends
the pines. And bends me back
to grasp of island and bay, back
to a different season
different day.

The mountains embrace my long-loved
mate, his story written on some hard-won
peak somewhere
that few even speak of anymore.

Water will hold my son's I think
as it's held him and holds him still.
His story has a ways to go, in baritone
and tenor notes that will rise
with every breath, I hope—
though I won't hear it sung.

Bone Is Bone

until it isn't

moth-chewed
worm-holed

no one can tell you
how long

no one can tell you
how well

you'll live
built as you are

rock maple
sweet sap

soured
sweat to ashes

bones to dust
blood is blood

until it's sickened
misshapen

deep in the marrow
we'll take

what's given
what's in the bone

tapped out
ticking

Day 403

403 days after the first COVID19 death in Washington State

& the avalanche lilies nod their heads
[a yellow mass in prayer] whisper / blissful /
unaware / to keep their distance

spring springs up regardless
of pandemic and politics
while we / impatient / watch

and wait for summer & promise
wait for MRI results / for someone
to touch / rain

what is promise if not something
to wait for / we answer
with our own solemn nods
six feet apart

summer's promise is born in tinder
on the shoulder of the mountain
& fire feels no fear / quivers

in its own quick flicker
of beauty / red-tail hawks
in tandem circle in tranquil ease
have no fear of our disease

sworn by habit to the wind / no reason
to pretend / anything is something
other than it is

◆

I'll Dress Myself in Wilderness and You

> *They were together in silence like an old married couple wary of life, beyond the pitfalls of passion, beyond the brutal mockery of hope and the phantoms of disillusion: beyond love.*
> —Gabriel García Márquez, Love in the Time of Cholera

What is this,
love, that keeps us
distant and alone,
keeps us together
but apart, you sleeping
in another room?
We both still gaze
into each other's
Facebook faces,
newsfeeds, status
updates. On the news
the pictures waver,
grim reports, masked
and unmasked, hidden
and in plain sight.
What is this
that feeds the solitary
soul so well
the chest tightens?
Let's make new
pacts, fresh urgings
before our human tissues
tense, our lungs refuse
to fill. I will dress myself
in wilderness, and you
will learn to dance.

Note: "Because Nothing Is Ever Finished"

Each line (including section titles) of this fifty-nine line poem is one line from each of the fifty-nine poems in Jane Hirshfield's *The October Palace* (copyright 1994, Harper Collins Publishers).

Because Nothing Is Ever Finished—*"History as the Painter Bonnard" pg 15*

They Opened, Because It Was Time and They Had No Choice—*"Narcissus: Tel Aviv, Baghdad, San Francisco, February 1991" pg 20*

They open their skin at first touch, yielding sweetness.—*"1973" pg 44*

Ripeness is what falls away with ease.—*"Ripeness" pg 78*

The mouth swallows peach and says gold.—*"The House in Winter" pg 11*

What enters, enters like that—unstoppable gift,—*"The Door" pg 40* because you taste it as you were meant to.—*"For a Wedding on Mount Tamalpais" pg 58*

Sunlight Never Reaches but the Earth Still Blooms—*"The Task" pg 65*

cobbled and rivered with all the green waters of earth,—*"This Love" pg 46*

the taste of things, cold and pure,—*"Each Step" pg 9*

the murmur of falling, the fluvial, purling wash—*"Percolation" pg 51*

the steep descent tasting of oceans,—*"Red Poppies" pg 8*

the merest trace of sorrow, remnant salt,—*"For the Autumn Dead: Election Day 1984" pg 22*

A shiver of crayon yellows and reds, of violet—*"The Mesmer" pg 59*

All day the world went on about its business.—*"The Hawk Cry" pg 33*

I must have missed it.—*"The Ritual" pg 28*

Even the silkworm's castings grew whiter, more strong.—*"In the Year Eight Hundred" pg 27*

For Fish, Water is Endless, for Birds, the Air—*"The Thief" pg 75*

open-winged for those moments between world and world.—*"Under the River" pg 60*

From glacier-lit blue to the gold of iguana, we name them, and naming, begin to see.—*"The Stone of Heaven" pg 89*

The same within them as without—*"The Shadow" pg 10*

And deep fish rise to feed as if some riddle—*"The Water Diamonds" pg 63*

assembled on thread so fine it is almost surmise,—*"Just Below the Surface" pg 77*

though a shadow flickers, remembering.—*"Of the Body" pg 74*

They are fish going on with their own concerns.—*"The
    Gods are not Large" pg 81*
Would Tenderness Wring the Heart Still of Its Burdens—
    "Even the Vanishing Housed" pg 67
yellow, plump, a little bruised?—*"The Groundfall Pear" pg 52*
The smooth and the scabbed, the wrinkled and lonely?—
    "At the Roosevelt Baths" pg 54
Each answer known before the question's asked.—
    "Courtship" pg 61
Ideas buzz the air like flies—*"Inspiration" pg 47*
a plentitude that binds.—*"A Plentitude" pg 18*
Again, the Wind Flakes Gold Leaf from the Trees—
    "Autumn" pg 37
as these falling needles and leaves speak of return.—
    "Leaving the October Palace" pg 76
The poor had returned to their hunger—*"A Recurring
    Possibility" pg 29*
more and more creased each year, worn paper-thin,—*"The
    Heart as Origami" pg 82*
each half-starved rib communicative as Braille,—*"The
    World" pg 30*
to be pounded down again, for what we've declared
    beautiful to be.—*"Floor" pg 32*
I too now wear that warning, and so pray—*"For a Gelding" pg
    64*
it is possible to cast yourself on the earth's good mercy
    and live,—*"Happiness" pg 45*
each of us pinned on the axis that spins out this dusk,—*"At
    Nightfall" pg 49*
the night's stampede of winds.—*"Storm: Yaddo 1989" pg 25*
Only the wild scent of the earth will be left—*"In Yellow
    Grass" pg 66*
and the angels look on, observing what falls: all of it
    falls.—*"The November Angels" pg 72*

Today, What Falls Is Wavering—*"What Falls" pg 38*
from the weight of too much seeing, too much seen.—
   "Cycladic Figure: the Harp Player" pg 13
Each time the found world surprises—that is its nature—
   "Meeting the Light Completely" pg 80
moving of shadows and grass—*"The Kingdom" pg 3*
in their sweetness and rustling.—*"Perceptibility Is a Kind of*
   Attentiveness" pg 23
Within this tree another tree—*"Within this Tree" pg 84*
Now see the dark-shelled flowers of thought unmade,—
   "The Wedding" pg 16
Whatever Asks, Heart Kneels and Offers to Bear—*"What*
   the Heart Wants" pg 7
But why does my heart look back at me, reproachful?—*"An*
   Earthly Beauty" pg 83
Fold that loneliness, one moment, two, love, back into
   your arms.—*"A Sweetening All Around Me as it Falls" pg 71*
Like new lovers taking their fill in the crowded dark,—
   "The Window" pg 87
their shadows' chiasmus will fleck and fill with flies.—*"The*
   Love of Aged Horses" pg 48
Such is the chaos that affection yields.—*"Empedocles' Physics"*
   pg 85
The heart's machinery starts up again, hammering and
   sawing—*"A Breakable Spell" pg 57*
humming of flies on their isinglass wings.—*"The Sting" pg*
   35
Then it asks more, and we give it.—*"The Weighing" pg 79*

Title Index

A

Another Home 47
Apology 27
A Sturdy Well-Built Home 74
A Thing That Breathes 13
At the end of February 80
Aubade 87

B

Because Nothing's Ever Finished 64
Bittersweet 48
Bone Is Bone 101

C

Cast 51
Cavern 73
Color Theory 96

D

Day 403 102
Dirge 53
Disembodiment 78

E
Edna Hid Walter from Us for Years 92
Elegy 23
Etude 19

F
Finding the Words 85
Flashpoint 49
Forecast 84

G
Ghazal to Breath 16
Ghazal to No One 77

H
Home and Here 89
Hopewell Bay 32
How Beautiful 86

I
I Couldn't Name What Can't Be Named 71
I'll Dress Myself in Wilderness and You 104
Instinct 44
Into the Wind 55

L
Leap of Faith 58
Let Me Swim 57

M
Me Too—the Fall of Man 28
My son is trying to forget himself 76

N
Nadeau Island, Shawanaga Bay 54
Not a Finch 70
Not as Beautiful 79
Not to Rise 59

O
One Story 93
Overseer 50

P
Passing through Blue Earth 61

S
Since the return of the massasauga 24
So Much Depends on Hunger 25
Sunflower 22
Surface Tension 95

T
That year 56
The Cicada Heat of Summer Is Upon Us 91
This Loud Heart 17
Today my son makes his first deep water dive 72
To My Mother While Listening to Stan Getz 97
Tonight, a blue moon rises 20

W
What I Want 99
What This House Knows 30
Wheatfield with Crows 21
Wrecked 60

First Line Index

Symbols

—a town in Minnesota 61
& the avalanche lilies nod their heads 102

A

a confession: I fell in love 32
All last night the wind 99
and it's been years 20
and remember himself as someone else 76
A road lay where you lay, broken 21

B

Because the end of the day looks like diamonds 71
body from body   water 78
But it's not a bat that batters in 44

C

Confused weather. Look out 84

D

death wintered over in me 56
Did they suffer? That is always the question 60

E

Each spring I watch the cowbird 73

F

Forgive me the need 28
For weeks we'd watched the white-headed male 74

H

His skin was scabrous bark and thick 50

I

I could start 17
I find the long braid while cleaning out a drawer 86
If the dying 57
In the Painted Hills 96
I see snakes everywhere. Any whir 24
I've been imagining my death 85
I watch you die 53

M

Mid-lake in midair 58
Mother, may I write of you now 97
Music's in my blood, they'd hear me say 19
My love   I don't know how   to tell you 27
My mother's father 92

N

No one there to see 23

O

On the paddle to Flat Rock, an island hanging 55

P

Pines here bend 54

R

Rotors thwap—a war zone here 47

S

scarlet berries, showy, constant 48
See how her face follows 22
Seventeen years 91

T

the child who so loved water,
   he didn't want to be born 72
The lake freezes, inhales, exhales, breathes 16
The ravens on my mantle 51
These are things you need to know 13
The sink attracts them 95
the storm has finally come 80
They open their skin at first touch,
   yielding sweetness 64
They said, and she believed, no one knew 77
They tell me my uterus 79
This house knows nothing 30
This morning, fog 89
This story starts in Toronto,
   where an orphaned son 93
Through the gag and cloy of spring 49

U

until it isn't 101
Up north 87

W

We are all born 25
What is this 104
What seeds take root in the
   crevices of your mind? 59

Y

Your son wants to be 70

www.ingramcontent.com/pod-product-compliance
Lightning Source LLC
Chambersburg PA
CBHW011947150426
43193CB00019B/2929